The ABC's of God

Answering Those What Is God Like
Questions With Your Children

Eric M. West

THE ABC'S OF GOD
Answering Those What Is God Like Questions With Your Children

ISBN (Paperback): 979-8-89672-219-9
ISBN (Hardback): 979-8-89672-220-5
ISBN (Ebook): 979-8-89672-221-2

PROMINENT
BOOKS
EDGE

5830 E 2nd St, Ste 7000 #9983
Casper, WY 82609
USA

DEDICATIONS

First of all I want to thank my Father in heaven, for loving me and giving me life. Thanks to the Lord Jesus Christ for demonstrating His love for us all, by paying the price for sin that we ourselves could never pay. I thank Him so much for His free gift of salvation. And I want to thank the Holy Spirit for watching over my life all these years and for sustaining me by His powerful word. God has been faithful to me every step of the way, from the time that I surrendered my life to Christ back in Watts, California, many years ago, to today; and I have full confidence that He will forever be faithful to anyone who put their trust in His son Jesus Christ. He has never abandoned me, and I pray that *The ABCs of God* will bring God glory wherever it goes.

To my adult children, whom I love very much, Ashley and Isaiah West. From the time I first held you both in my arms, I prayed for you that you will both come to know the Savior, Jesus Christ, as your personal savior; and that prayer has been answered. May you continue to grow as adults becoming the people who God made you to be. The happiest time of my life was spent helping to raise you with your mom. I love you forever.

And to my grandkids, Jackson, Jetson, Jameson, and my first and only granddaughter, Jasmine. Thanks for letting Papa use your hands for the cover of this book. I wrote this for you because I wanted to add my part in introducing you to your Creator. As you get older, may this book serve as an aid to introduce you as to Who He is. You were each made to know Him and to bring Him glory. May God someday grant you the hunger and thirst to know Him, His character, and His great love for you.

Always remember this: Jesus Christ is the greatest love you will ever know, for this is where your value will be truly realized as you come to personally trust in Him. Your parents and your grandparents love you forever.

ACKNOWLEDGEMENTS

To my daughter Ashley, it was you who gave me the idea to publish *The ABCs of God*, selflessly encouraging me to share this book with other kids too rather than just your own. Your excitement for the devotional, as it was intended to be, truly inspired me, and I thank you and love you for it.

I want to thank the children at Central Christian Academy in Wichita, Kansas, for allowing me to illustrate my book with your artwork. And to those whose art was not selected, not because your work wasn't just as valued, but because I was limited as to how many drawings I could have in the book. Thank you as well. Wherever God takes this book, *The ABCs of God*, your beautiful pictures will go with it, and together, we will glorify God through it.

Thank you to David Landis, headmaster at Central Christian Academy, for supporting the idea of the book and for allowing the kids who participated to do their work during classroom hours.

Thanks to Mrs. Jayme Davis, director of Advancement at Central Christian Academy, for the joy that you shared with the book and for communicating with the parents of the kids to get them on board. Thank you!

I want to thank Ms. Brenda Cooper, Elementary Art, for facilitating the kids' artwork and using part of your class time at that. You were such an encouragement to me, and I thank you for lending me your palm print suggestions for the book's cover. A thank-you to Mrs. Evelyn Moore, Middle School Art, for letting a few of your students participate with their artwork as well. You were very supportive also, and I thank you.

A

Bible verse:

"O' LORD God ALMIGHTY, who is like you? You are mighty, O' LORD, and your faithfulness surrounds you." (Psalm 89:8)

My Thoughts:

No one is like God.

What are your thoughts?

by Stella Garwood
4th Grade

B

Bible verse:

"The LORD gives strength to His people; the Lord BLESSES His people with His peace." (Psalm 29:11)

Thoughts:

God loves to bless His people.

What are your thoughts?

by Olivia Kallenberger
4th Grade

C

Bible verse:

"In the beginning God CREATED the heavens
and the earth." (Genesis 1:1)

Thoughts:

Everything was made by God, including man and woman, the Earth
and the universe. He is our creator.

What are your thoughts?

by Braylon Salter
4th Grade

6

D

Bible verse:

"For the LORD takes DELIGHT in His people; He crowns the humble with salvation." (Psalm 149:4)

Thoughts:

God looks forward to being there for us. He alone can save us.

What are your thoughts?

by Jackson Eisel
4th Grade

8

Bible verse:

"Your word, O LORD, is ETERNAL; it stands firm in the heavens."

Thoughts:

The Word of God will last forever. It will never end.

What are your thoughts?

9

by Ryker Ross
4th Grade

10

F

Bible verse:

"The LORD is FAITHFUL to all of His promises and loving toward all He has made." (Psalm 145:13b)

Thoughts:

God can be trusted. He never breaks His promises.

What are your thoughts?

11

by F. Ani Doom/Cooper Pendergrass
Middle School

12

G

Bible verse:

The LORD is **GOOD** to all; He has compassion
on all He has made." (Psalm 145:9)

Thoughts:

God is a good God. He desires to do good to all He has made.

What are your thoughts?

13

love God, love people

by Mark Oswald
4th Grade

Bible verse:

"Day and night they never stop saying: HOLY, HOLY, HOLY, is the Lord God Almighty, who was, and is, and is to come." (Revelation 4:8b)

Thoughts:

God stands alone; no one is like Him, and He deserves our praise.

What are your thoughts?

by Lily Baldesarre
4th Grade

16

I

Bible verse:

"For nothing is IMPOSSIBLE with God." (Luke 1:37)

Thoughts:

God can do anything He wants to do. He always does what is right and true.

What are your thoughts?

IMPOSSIBLE

true and right

by Jenna Seaman
4th Grade

18

J

Bible verse:

"For God will bring every deed into JUDGMENT, including every hidden thing, whether good or bad." (Ecclesiastes 12:14)

Thoughts:

God sees everything, and nothing gets past Him at all. Be honest with Him now.

What are your thoughts?

Paige♡

2-B

by Page Fiscus
3rd Grade

K

Bible verse:

"I will tell of the KINDNESS of the LORD, the deeds which He is to be praised, according to all the LORD has done." (Isaiah 63:7a)

Thoughts:

God loves to show kindness to His people.

What are your thoughts?

by Quin Heater
3rd Grade

L

Bible verse:

"For God so LOVED the world, that He gave His only Son, that whoever believes in Him should not perish but have eternal life." (John 3:16)

Thoughts:

God provided a way for us to be saved from our sins so we can live with Him forever.

What are your thoughts?

23

by Isabella Wawrzweski
4th Grade

M

Bible verse:

"Remember, O LORD, your great MERCY and love,
for they are from of old." (Psalm 25:6)

Thoughts:

God wants to show us mercy.

What are your thoughts?

25

by Kate Oswald
3rd Grade

26

N

Bible verse:

"A Psalm of David. Bless the LORD, O my soul, and all that is within me, bless His holy NAME." (Psalm 103:1)

Thoughts:

God's name is worthy of our praise.

What are your thoughts?

by Shay Davis
4th Grade

O

Bible verse:

"Your eyes saw my unformed body. All the days ORDAINED for me were written in your book before one of them came to be." (Psalm 139:16)

Thoughts:

God has given us a certain amount of days on Earth. He is in control.

What are your thoughts?

by Wyatt Sauer
4th Grade

wyat 3b

P

Bible verse:

"May God Himself, the God of PEACE sanctify you through and through. May your whole spirit, soul, and body be kept blameless at the coming of our Lord Jesus Christ." (1 Thessalonians 5:23)

Thoughts:

God's peace brings healing to our souls because He loves us.

What are your thoughts?

by Olivia Calvert
4th Grade

Q

Bible verse:

"For since the creation of the world, God's visible QUALITIES—
His eternal power and divine nature—have been clearly
seen, so that men are without excuse." (Romans 1:20)

Thoughts:

God's fingerprints are all over creation. Proof of His existence is
everywhere.

What are your thoughts?

by Elle Samuelson
3rd Grade

R

Bible verse:

"The Lord is RIGHTEOUS in all His ways and loving
toward all He has made." (Psalm 145:17)

Thoughts:

God's nature is righteous and good. He always does what is right.

What are your thoughts?

by Lainie Harper
3rd Grade

36

S

Bible verse:

"I, even I, am the LORD, and apart from me there is no SAVIOR." (Isaiah 43:11)

Thoughts:

God declares Himself as the only Savior.

What are your thoughts?

37

by Corra Shideler
4th Grade

T

Bible verse:

"For my THOUGHTS are not your thoughts, neither are your ways my ways, saith the Lord." (Isaiah 55:8)

Thoughts:

God doesn't think like we think. His thoughts are way bigger than ours, and His ways are far better than ours.

What are your thoughts?

by Kaniah Morsee
4th Grade

U

Bible verse:

"The Lord delights in those who fear Him, who put their hope in His UNFAILING love." (Psalm 147:11)

Thoughts:

God know He is faithful, but He wants us to put our trust in Him.

What are your thoughts?

41

by Johanna Terronez
Middle School

42

V

Bible verse:

"But thanks be to God! He gives us the VICTORY through our Lord Jesus Christ." (1 Corinthians 15:57)

Thoughts:

God is a victorious God, and He gives us victory to through His Son, Jesus Christ.

What are your thoughts?

43

VICTORY

by Lily Baldesarre
4th Grade

44

W

Bible verse:

"Every WORD of God is flawless; He is a shield to those who take refuge in Him." (Proverbs 30:5)

Thoughts:

God can not lie; He keeps His promises, and He cannot make mistakes.

What are your thoughts?

45

Every word
of God is
flawless; He
is a shield
to those
who take
refuge in
him
Proverbs 30:5

by Braylon Salter
4th Grade

X

Bible verse:

"Be EXALTED, O God, above the heavens; let your glory be over all the earth." (Psalm 57:11)

Thoughts:

God is higher than all the stars of heaven; no one is greater.

What are your thoughts?

EXALTED

by Lily Baldesarre
4th Grade

Bible verse:

"Jesus Christ is the same YESTERDAY and today and forever." (Hebrews 13:8)

Thoughts:

Jesus can always be trusted because He does not change like people do.

What are your thoughts?

Yesterday

by Katie Fiscus
4th Grade

Z

Bible verse:

"Then you will know that I, the Lord your God,
dwell in ZION, my holy hill." (Joel 3:17a)

Thoughts:

Zion is very important to God. Zion is another name for Jerusalem.

What are your thoughts?

by Titus Murphy
4th Grade

52

ABOUT THE AUTHOR

I was born in Pine Bluff, Arkansas, but was raised in the inner city of Watts, California. I met this inner-city ministry called World Impact, which came into the Imperial Courts Housing Projects each week, beginning shortly after the Watts riots of 1965, to minister to children and families. I gave my life to Christ that first week in LA. But the Crips and Blood gangs had grown widespread across Los Angeles by that time, and due to that pressure and others, I soon came to believe that God didn't care about me, resulting from all my unanswered questions and being physically abused by my peers. Authority became negative to me, and I soon rebelled against my stepfather's authority—and God's.

I joined the Grape Street Watts Crips gang at age twelve and co-founded a clique within Grape called the Watts Baby Loc's with my best friend Edward Robinson, who is now with the Lord. After eight years in that lifestyle, God saw fit to rescue me from suicide, and I committed my life to Jesus Christ. After a year of discipleship through World Impact, I accepted an opportunity to join World Impact's Christian Leadership Training Center in their two-year program, in Florence, Kansas. After graduating from there, I joined World Impact staff in Wichita, Kansas, where I would meet my wife, Andrea, a math teacher. God blessed us with two children, Ashley and Isaiah West, and Ashley gave us four beautiful grandchildren, Jackson, Jetson, Jameson, and one granddaughter Jasmine.

I work at Central Christian Church in maintenance for the last twenty-six years. I wrote my autobiography *From Crip To Christ* and have been featured on Pacific Garden Missions radio drama program *UNSHACKLED*. God has made me a mentor to young men, which has been an honor for me.

"But whoever causes one of these little ones who believe in Me to sin, it would be better for him if a millstone were hung around his neck, and he were drowned in the depth of the sea." {Matt.18:6, NKJV)

Why I Chose to Write *The ABCs of God*?

I decided to write this book because three years or so ago, my daughter had decided to move to Arkansas. Up until that point, I had been a constant male influence in my two oldest grandsons' lives, Jackson and Jetson. I used to get them just about every weekend. I loved taking them outside on walks, picking up pine cones, looking at different bugs, or whatever they wanted to do out there, we pretty much did. We would throw the football around, play basketball, and before bed, I continued a routine that I had once done with their mom Ashley and Uncle Isaiah. After they had taken their baths, we would pop popcorn and grab some snacks and sit and watch *Veggie Tales* or the Bible series *Superbook* until it was time to pray, and then I'll put them down for the night.

But when my daughter Ashley told me that they were moving to Arkansas, that did something to me. It was a hard pill to swallow, but I respected her decision. I wanted to somehow continue that godly influence for Christ in their lives, so God gave me an idea, assuming it was from Him, to do a little devotional that she can read to them. The idea to use the alphabets to describe how God is and what He is like just popped into my head. So I got a notebook from Walmart and found different verses that describe different attributes or character qualities of God.

The late A. W. Tozer wrote a book called *The Attributes of God*. It was a model for me, but by way of the use of the alphabets for children. When I finished it, I mailed it off to my daughter because they had left by the time I finished it. When she got it and looked over it, she called and said, "Dad, I love it! You should publish it and make it available for other kids too." I thought that was selfless of her. So I prayed about it, and God impressed on my heart to do it, and today, the reality of that dream is in your hands.

Matthew 19:13–14 says, "Then people brought little children to Jesus for him to place his hands on them and pray for them. But the disciples rebuked them. Jesus said, 'Let the little children come to me, and do not hinder them, for the kingdom of heaven belongs to such as these'" (NIV).

In another passage, Jesus says, "But whoever causes one of these little ones who believe in Me to sin, it would be better for him if a millstone were hung around his neck, and drowned in the depth of the sea." -Matt.18:6, NKJV. Jesus takes children very seriously, and He has an issue with people preventing children from knowing Him as well, and I understand that and know the advantage for teaching them about God while they are young. And because I was exposed to God early on in my life by my grandmother and the World Impact ministries, based out of Los Angeles when I was threatening to end my life as a teenager, God was able to bring to memory what I was taught about Jesus as a child, and He was able to save my life both physically and spiritually.

You never know how God will use His powerful word in their lives later on. The greatest gift that we can give our kids and grandkids is the knowledge of who God is, and the Savior Jesus Christ. This is why I wrote *The ABCs of God* for my grandchildren, which, since then, two more grandchildren have been born, Jameson and Jasmine.

I hope this book blesses you and your family as well.

God bless!